Contents

ADHD AND AUTISM

INTRODUCTION

Attention deficit hyperactivity disorder (ADHD) and autism can look a lot like each other. Children with either condition can have problems focusing. They can be impulsive or have a hard time communicating. They may have trouble with schoolwork and with relationships.

Although they share many of the same symptoms, the two are distinct conditions. Autism spectrum disorders are a series of related developmental disorders that can affect language skills, behavior, social interactions, and the ability to learn. ADHD impacts the way the brain grows and develops. And you can have both.

The correct diagnosis early on helps children get the right treatment so they don't miss out on important development and learning. People with these conditions can have successful, happy lives.

How Are They Different?

Keep an eye on how your child pays attention. Those with autism struggle to focus on things that they don't like, such as reading a book or doing a puzzle. And they may fixate on things that they do like, such as playing with a particular toy. Kids with ADHD dislike and avoid things they'll have to concentrate on.

You should also study how your child is learning to communicate. Although kids with either condition struggle to interact with others, those with autism have less social awareness of others around them. They often have a hard time putting words to their thoughts and feelings, and they may not be able to point to an object to give meaning to their speech. They find it hard to make eye contact.

A child with ADHD, on the other hand, may talk nonstop. They're more likely to interrupt when someone else is speaking or butt in and try to monopolize a conversation. Also, consider the subject. Some kids with autism can talk for hour's about a topic that they're interested in.

An autistic child loves order and repetition, but one with ADHD doesn't, even if it helps them. A child with autism might want the same type of food at a favorite restaurant, for instance, or become overly attached to one toy or shirt. They'll become upset when routines change. A child with ADHD doesn't like doing the same thing again or for long times.

ADHD- and ASD-specific behaviors

Often, children with ADHD have difficulty focusing on one activity or task. When they are engaged in their daily activities they may be easily distracted. It is challenging for children with ADHD to complete one task before jumping to another, and they are often physically unable to sit still. But some children with ADHD may be so interested in a topic or activity that they fixate on it, or hyperfocus. Although focusing on one thing can be positive, it may mean that children have difficulty moving their attention to other activities when they are asked to do so.

Children with ASD are most likely to be overfocused, unable to shift their attention to the next task. They are often inflexible when it comes to their routines, with low tolerance for change. That may mean taking the same route and eating the same things every day. Many are highly sensitive or insensitive to light, noise, touch, pain, smell, or taste or have a strong interest in them. They may have set food preferences based on color or texture and may make gestures such as repeated hand flapping. Their intense focus means people with ASD are often able to remember detailed facts for a long time and may be particularly good at math, science, art, and music.

Symptoms of ADHD and autism

In the earliest stages, it's not unusual for ADHD and ASD to be mistaken for the other. Children with either condition may experience trouble communicating and focusing. Although they have some similarities, they're still two distinct conditions.

Here's a comparison of the two conditions and their symptoms:

ADHD symptoms Autism symptoms

Being easily distracted ✓

Frequently jumping from one task to another or quickly growing bored with tasks ✓

Unresponsive to common stimuli ✓

Difficulty focusing, or concentrating and narrowing attention to one task ✓

Intense focus and concentration on a singular item ✓

Talking nonstop or blurting things out ✓

Hyperactivity✓

Trouble sitting still ✓

Interrupting conversations or activities ✓

Lack of concern or inability to react to other people's emotions or feelings ✓✓

Repetitive movement, such as rocking or twisting ✓

Avoiding eye contact ✓

Withdrawnbehaviors ✓

Impaired social interaction ✓

Delayed developmental milestones ✓

When they occur together

There may be a reason why symptoms of ADHD and ASD can be difficult to distinguish from one another. Both can occur at the same time.

Not every child can be clearly diagnosed. A doctor may decide only one of the disorders is responsible for your child's symptoms. In other cases, children may have both conditions.

According to the Centers for Disease Control and Prevention (CDC), 14 percentTrusted Source of children with ADHD also have ASD. In one study from 2013, children with both conditions had more debilitating symptoms than children who didn't exhibit ASD traits.

In other words, children with ADHD and ASD symptoms were more likely to have learning difficulties and impaired social skills than children who only had one of the conditions.

Understanding the combination

For many years, doctors were hesitant to diagnose a child with both ADHD and ASD. For that reason, very few medical studies have looked at the impact of the combination of conditions on children and adults.

The American Psychiatric Association (APA) stated for years that the two conditions couldn't be diagnosed in the same person. In 2013, the APA changed its stanceTrusted Source. With the release of the Diagnostic and Statistical Manual of Mental Disorders, Fifth Edition (DSM-5), the APA states that the two conditions can co-occur.

In a 2014 review of studies looking at the co-occurrence of ADHD and ASD, researchers found that between 30 to 50 percent of people with ASD also have symptoms of ADHD. Researchers don't fully understand the cause for either condition, or why they occur together so frequently.

Both conditions may be linked to genetics. One study identified a rare gene that may be linked to both conditions. This finding could explain why these conditions often occur in the same person.

More research is still needed to better understand the connection between ADHD and ASD.

How To Diagnosis

If you think your child has either ADHD or autism, talk to your doctor about what testing you'll need. There's no one thing that can say whether a child has either condition, or both. You can start with your pediatrician, who may refer you to a specialist.

To diagnose ADHD, doctors look for a pattern of behaviors over time like being distracted or forgetful, not following through, having trouble waiting for a turn, and fidgeting or squirming. They'll ask for feedback from parents, teachers, and other adults that care for the child. A doctor will also try to rule out other possible causes for the symptoms.

An autism diagnosis starts with a parent answering a questionnaire about the child, often about behaviors that started when they were very young. Further tests and tools may include more questionnaires, surveys, and checklists, as well as interviews and observed activities.

Treatments for Autism and ADHD

While the symptoms of ADHD generally respond well to the most commonly prescribed medications, ASD symptoms are less likely to do so. Symptoms of ASD that often overlap with ADHD, such as hyperactivity, impulsiveness, and inattention, may respond to the medications used to treat ADHD, if not as well. Medications to treat ASD are now being developed, and irritability, aggression, and self-injury that are related to ASD usually respond to antipsychotic medications.

Medication is frequently part of the treatment plan for children with ADHD because it helps reduce some of the major symptoms, including hyperactivity and impulsivity. The most commonly prescribed medications are methylphenidate (Ritalin, Concerta, Metadate, Quillivant), amphetamine (Adderall, Dexedrine, Vyvanse, Dyanavel), atomoxetine (Strattera), and guanfacine (Intuniv, Tenex). However, when they are used to treat patients with both ADHD and ASD, the stimulants—methylphenidate and amphetamine—seem less effective and cause more side effects, including social withdrawal, depression, and irritability, than when they are used to treat ADHD alone.

ADHD and Your Child's Social Life

Making friends isn't always easy for a kid with ADHD. What can a parent do to help? Quite a bit.

Treat the ADHD. The same treatments that help your child succeed in school can also help with social issues. Medicine can also cut down on behaviors like impulsiveness that may keep other kids away.

Make introductions. If your child is nervous about talking to classmates, set up play dates. Plan activities ahead of time, and be there to keep an eye on things.

It may help to choose something fun that your child is comfortable doing. This will encourage confidence. Keep in mind that kids with ADHD tend to do better with one or two other children than in large groups.

Talk first. Before your child goes to an event, talk about what they should expect there, and what others might expect from them.

Get active. Look for hobbies that center around your child's interests. It can be things like art, video games, sports, or whatever. Instead of signing up for what you think is best, let your child help you decide. Look for programs that have kids with ADHD in mind.

Focus. Don't try to do too much at once. Pick one or two habits to work on with them at a time, such as taking turns or sharing.

Explore social skills groups. There are programs designed to help your child learn to make friends and do better in class. A school psychologist or speech therapist usually leads them. They're also small. Typically, there aren't more than eight kids in a group.

The children in these sessions do special activities, like role-playing, to learn how to:

Greet other kids

Start and hold a conversation

Take turns when playing

Ask for help when they need it

Many schools have these groups. There are also privately run programs. The key is to find one that fits your child's personality and age group.

Have a backup plan. Ask your child's teachers how class is going for them Work with them and the school's guidance counselor to clear up any conflicts that could get in the way of friendships.

Kids with ADHD can be targets for bullying, too. Be prepared. Talk with your child about what to do if they get teased or picked on. Make sure they know it's OK to tell you if they are bullied.

Know that a little may be enough. Remember, while you want to encourage friendships, don't go overboard. Your child doesn't need to be part of the most popular group at school or have lots of friends. One or two close friendships may be all they need.

Can You Prevent ADHD?

Though there is no way to prevent ADHD , there are ways to help all children feel and do their best at home and at school.

Can good prenatal care help to prevent ADHD?

Complications of pregnancy are linked to ADHD. You can increase the chance of your child not having ADHD by staying healthy throughout yourpregnancy. A healthy diet and regular doctor visits are important. So is avoiding the use of alcohol and drugs.

Children whose mothers smoked while they were pregnant are twice as likely to develop ADHD. Some studies suggest a pregnant woman's exposure to lead, as well as lead exposure in early childhood, may be linked to ADHD. Other studies are exploring the possible connection between premature birth and ADHD.

Does diet play a role in preventing ADHD?

Giving your child a healthy, balanced diet from an early age is good for all children, whether or not they have ADHD.

Some experts believe that altering a child's diet may reduce hyperactive behavior. Ben Feingold developed a popular diet designed to lessen hyperactivity. It is an elimination diet that targets artificial colorings, flavorings, and preservatives. The medical community hasn't accepted the diet, and some studies have disproved Feingold's theory. Still, many parents who have tried the diet reported an improvement in their child's behavior.

There is no scientific proof linking ADHD to sugar. Processed sugars and carbohydrates may affect a child's activity level by rapidly raising blood sugar levels. This blood sugar spike may produce an adrenaline rush that could cause a child to become more active, followed by a "crash" in activity and mood as the adrenaline levels fall.

Parents are encouraged to try cutting certain foods from their children's diet if they feel the foods affect behavior negatively. It's usually best to eliminate one food or category at a time so that you can be certain the effect you are seeing can be attributed to the category you are eliminating. Some experts, though, think that behavioral changes may be due to the way the families interact with each other while they're on an elimination diet. The child's behavior may improve -- not because of the diet, but as a result of getting more attention from the parents.

It's important not to go too far. Being too restrictive with your child's diet can lead to nutritional deficiencies. Dietitians and doctors can help you make a healthy eating plan for your children.

Its important to weigh the risks and benefits of elimination diets, particularly for children who may be experiencing decreased appetite as a side effect of many medications commonly used to treat ADHD.

Can structured routine help in preventing ADHD?

All children, and especially those with ADHD, can benefit from structured routines and clear expectations.

Post a daily schedule where your child can see it, so they know what to expect. This daily schedule should include specific times for such activities as:

Waking up

Eating meals

Playing

Doing homework

Doing chores

Watching TV

Taking part in after-school activities

Going to bed

Once the schedule is set, follow it as closely as possible each day. If there are going to be any disruptions in the schedule, explain them in advance to your child. Though posting a schedule doesn't prevent ADHD, it should help improve your child's ability to stay on task.

For older children, with or without ADHD, having a homework routine in place can make the after-school time more effective. Set aside an area away from distractions for doing homework. Taking small breaks during homework time can also help, especially if your child is hyperactive and has difficulty staying focused.

How does behavior management help in preventing ADHD?

Many therapists believe you can impact your child's behavior by using behavior management.

The first step is to foster a positive parent-child relationship. Therapists say this can be done by spending quality time with your child each day -- your child's "special time." During this time, let them pick an activity. Then simply focus on enjoying your child and their interests.

The next step in behavioral management is to use positive reinforcement when your child behaves well. Praise and reward them for it. Your child may behave well more often. Experts encourage parents to notice their child's good behavior at least five times a day and offer simple praise for it.

Keep your expectations reasonable. Base them on what's appropriate for your child's age and focus on only a few tasks at a time. Clearly explain what type of behavior you expect from your child in order to be rewarded. If you think of several appropriate rewards and let your child pick from among them, they may take more ownership in the program. That will make success more likely.

It's important for your child to know what you expect. One way to do that is to look into their eyes when you talk to them. Then make all directions very specific, simple, and concise, and explain them in a calm voice. You can have your child repeat the directions back to you to make sure they understand.

Finally, it is very important that you be consistent. If you don't always reward good behavior, for example, it sends your child mixed messages.

If your child's teacher is using a behavior or reward system at school, try to implement a similar system at home. Many teachers use points, stickers, or color-level systems to reward good behavior.

Will using negative consequences change behavior?

The last step in behavioral management is providing negative consequences for bad behavior.

Once again, it is important to explain bad behavior to your child clearly. That way you can make sure they understand what is expected.

Start by explaining what's acceptable and what the reward is for that behavior. Then explain the negative consequences for bad behavior.

Be consistent. Don't be too harsh. Using negative consequences for unacceptable behavior is controversial, and negative consequences should never be cruel, abusive, or a reflection of your own emotions, no matter how frustrated you may feel.

For behavior therapy to work, give children with ADHD frequent reminders of expected behavior and consequences. One way to do this is to write down the rules, consequences, and rewards. Then put them in a place where your child can see them.For younger children you can draw pictures or print images for a more visual reminder.

Children with ADHD also need frequent feedback about their progress. They may do better with short-term goals rather than long-term ones. Keep changing the reward system so they don't get bored.

Start Teaching Attention Skills Early

If you have a preschooler, play games, build with blocks, and do puzzles together. It's good practice for building attention skills. Reading to your child is another good way to teach them how to pay attention. Showing them lots of affection can also help a child calm down and pay attention.

Not everyone agrees, but some experts think that television watching can hinder a child's ability to learn to pay attention. Regardless of whether or not TV causes attention deficiencies, the American Academy of Pediatrics says children younger than 18 months should watch very little TV. The academy also says that between the ages of 2 and 5, they should watch no more than 1 hour a day. Video chatting for toddlers/babies is generally considered to be OK at any age.

How Is ADHD Diagnosed?

ADHD is a complex condition and is sometimes difficult to diagnose.

There is no single test for ADHD. Doctors diagnose ADHD in children and teens after discussing symptoms at length with the child, parents, and teachers and observing the child's behaviors. The doctor will also gather information about any similar problems that run in the family and consider all possible causes.

To confirm a diagnosis of ADHD or learning differences, a battery of tests may be given to assess a child's neurological and psychological status. The tests should be given by a pediatrician or mental health provider with experience in diagnosing and treating ADHD. The tests include:

A medical and social history of both the child and the family.

A physical exam and neurological assessment that includes screenings of vision, hearing, and verbal and motor skills.

More tests may be given if there is a possibility that hyperactivity is related to some other physical problem.

An evaluation of intelligence, aptitude, personality traits, or processing skills. These evaluations are often done with input from the parents and teachers if the child is of school age.

A scan, called the Neuropsychiatric EEG-Based Assessment Aid (NEBA) System, that measures theta and beta brain waves. The theta/beta ratio has been shown to be higher in children and adolescents with ADHD than in children without it.

What Are the Treatments for ADHD?

The most effective treatment for ADHD is thought to be a combination of medication and psychological and behavioral therapies. Close cooperation among therapists, doctors, teachers, and parents is very important, and team meetings help.

Stimulants. Although there is considerable controversy about their possible overuse, stimulants are the most commonly prescribed medications for treating ADHD. Stimulants often decrease hyperactivity and improve concentration. They includeamphetamine salt combo (Adderall, Adderall XR), dexmethylphenidate (Focalin, Focalin XR), dextroamphetamine (Dexedrine), lisdexamfetamine (Vyvanse), methylphenidate (Concerta, Daytrana, Jornay PM, Metadate, Methylin, Ritalin, Quillichew, Quillivant XR), and and mixed salts of a single-entity amphetamine product (Mydayis). The newest formulations allow children to take the medicine only once a day. Jornay PM is taken in the evening ebfore bedtme. Daytrana is a methylphenidate-based medication that comes in the form of a skin patch that is applied once a day and worn for about 9 hours. The patch has been known to cause skin irritation and even permanent skin discoloration so should be monitored.

A doctor needs to monitor the dosage of the stimulant medication closely, both to determine the most effective level of drug and to watch for any side effects. Generally, most side effects of stimulants are mild and may include decreased appetite, stomach aches, sleep problems, headaches, and an increase in anxiety .

However, in rare cases, stimulants can have more serious side effects. For instance, some are linked to a higher risk of heart problems and sudden death in children with preexisting heart disease. They may also worsen psychiatric conditions like depression or anxiety or cause a psychotic reaction in some individuals. Before your kids start taking an ADHD medicine, talk to your doctor about the risks and benefits.

Non-stimulants. Atomoxetine (Strattera) and clonidine (Catapres and Kapvay) are two non-stimulant drugs for ADHD. Another drug similar to clonidine, approved for children aged 6 to 17, is guanfacine (Intuniv), which uses the same active ingredient as guanfacine hydrochloride

(Tenex), ablood pressuremedicine that has been used as an ADHD treatment.

Of course, these drugs have their own side effects and risks, and your doctor will want to watch for problems. In 2005, the FDA issued a public health advisory about rare reports of suicidal thinking in children and adolescents taking Strattera.

Other drugs. In some cases, doctors may try prescribing other antidepressant medications, such as drugs called SSRIs, bupropion (Wellbutrin), venlafaxine (Effexor) or others.

Psychological therapy. Of the psychological therapies, behavior modification may be the most commonly recommended for children. It can be quite effective, particularly if the therapist helps parents learn techniques to help the child's behavior. It is often combined with specific educational interventions, such as help with learning skills. Psychotherapy, including cognitive behavioral therapy is a valuable option, particularly if the child has low self-esteem, depression or anxiety.

ADHD Multimodal Treatment

ADHD (attention deficit hyperactivity disorder) is characterized by inattention, hyperactivity, and the inability to control impulses. It affects an estimated 5.2 million school-age children in the U.S.

Everyone, especially younger children, may have symptoms of ADHD from time to time. But with ADHD, the ability to function with daily activities is affected. A diagnosis of ADHD can be hard to make, and evaluation must be made by a specialist.

There are several different approaches to treating ADHD. But research suggests that for many children, the best way to manage the symptoms is a multimodal approach.

What Is a Multimodal Approach to Treating ADHD?

Multimodal treatment involves multiple methods of treatment that work together to help a child with ADHD.

The main components of this approach are medications, behavioral therapy, and education.

Medications and ADHD

The most commonly prescribed medications for ADHD are stimulants. These include:

Amphetamine (Adzenys XR-ODT)

Amphetamine/Dextroamphetamine (Adderall, Adderall XR)

Dexmethylphenidate (Focalin, Focalin XR)

Dextroamphetamine (Dexedrine or Dextrostat)

Lisdexamfetamine (Vyvanse)

Methylphenidate (Concerta, Daytrana, Metadate, Methylin, Quillivant XR, Ritalin)

Some of these medications are available in long or short acting formulations.

Non-stimulant medications used to treat ADHD, include:

Atomoxetine (Strattera)

Clonidine ER (Kapvay)

Guanfacine ER (Intuniv)

ADHD medications are used to improve children's ability to concentrate and work. Sometimes, a doctor must prescribe different medications or different dosages before finding the best treatment for a child. Doctors and parents need to carefully monitor children taking medications for ADHD.

Side effects of ADHD medicines can include

Anxiety

Decreased appetite

Fatigue

Irritability

Sleeping difficulties

Skin discoloration (with patches)

Upset stomach

Most side effects are minor and improve with time. In some cases, doctors may lower a medication dosage to relieve side effects.

The FDA recommends that a thorough medical history and exam, including an evaluation of underlying heart or psychiatric problems, be done as part of an ADHD treatment plan. A higher risk of strokes, heart attacks, and sudden death among patients with existing heart conditions has been linked to use of ADHD medications. An increased risk of psychiatric problems has also been linked to ADHD medications.

Medical Devices and ADHD

The FDA has recently given approval to a device called Monarch external Trigeminal Nerve Stimulation (eTNS) System to treat children age 7 to 12 years old. the cell phone-sized device delivers mild stimulation to electrodes which are attached to a patch worn on the patient's forehead. Those electrical pulses interact with the part of the brain which is believed to be responsible for ADHD.

Behavioral Therapy and ADHD

Behavioral therapy is designed to help a child curb problematic behaviors. This may involve helping the child learn to organize time and activities. Or it could help a child complete homework. It may also involve helping the child control their impulses and responses to emotional stimuli.

Education and ADHD

Educating parents about the disorder and its management is another important part of ADHD treatment. For parents, this may include learning parenting skills to help the child manage their behavior. That would involve skills such as giving positive feedback for desirable behaviors, ignoring undesirable behaviors, and giving time-outs when the child's behavior is out of control. In some cases, the child's entire family may be involved in this part of the treatment.

The Benefits of Multimodal Treatment

Treatment guidelines call for behavior therapy as the preferred treatment for preschool children with ADHD. Medicine may be prescribed if further treatment is needed. For older children with ADHD, age 6 and older, an approach that includes both behavior therapy and medication is preferred.

Researchers have found that multimodal treatment was particularly effective for improving social skills in children in highly stressful environments. It also was effective for those with anxiety and depression in addition to ADHD.

Children who receive multimodal treatment may need lower doses of medications compared to children only receiving medication.

Individualized Treatment Plan

A multimodal plan is effective for most children. The particular therapy and medication, however, will vary depending on the individual child. Doctors, parents, and teachers need to work together to develop and administer the best treatment for each child and family.

ADHD Drugs: How to Handle Side Effects in Kids

The right medicine can help kids with ADHD (attention deficit hyperactivity disorder) focus so they can finish homework and other tasks. It also can help them fidget less and have better social skills.

But ADHD drugs also have side effects that can be hard on kids -- and their parents.

It can take some trial and error to find the right drug and the right dose for your child. And even when you find the right combination, there may still be some side effects.

Keep track of how the medication affects your child so you can tell the doctor. If they're causing serious problems, a new medication or different dose may be tried.

These tips can help you both deal with some of the most common side effects.

Loss of Appetite

Children need a healthy, balanced diet to grow and develop the way they should. When ADHD drugs make them less hungry, they may not get enough calories, vitamins, and other nutrients. Some things you can try:

Give them healthy breakfast and dinner. When children aren't hungry at lunch, they may skip it, or they may try a light snack (crackers, cheese stick, fruit).That makes morning and evening meals extra important.

Try a shorter-acting drug. Long-acting drugs, sometimes called extended release, can last all day. Shorter-acting drugs can wear off in 3 to 4 hours -- just in time for meals.

Take a mini-break from medication. Ask your doctor if your child can skip medication for short periods of time, like on weekends, school holidays and breaks or before special-occasion meals.

If possible give medication with breakfast, not before.

Allow a bedtime snack that makes up for the skipped lunch.

Sleep Problems

ADHD drugs can keep kids up at night. That can happen if they took the last dose of the day too close to bedtime. Or it could be that a long-acting drug hasn't worn off by bedtime. But you might wait a few weeks before asking your child's doctor if you should make any changes to the medication. In the interim, make sure that your child isn't taking the afternoon dose too close to bedtime, and make sure your child has some activity after school to get rid of all the wiggles and energy. Sleep problems caused by ADHD medicine tend to get better with time.

And keep in mind that overstimulation -- not medicine -- may be behind your child's sleep problems. It can help to keep them off video games and their phone or computer before bedtime. You might try these other tips, too:

Make the room sleep-friendly. Light tells your body it's time to be up, so a dark room is important. Turn on a fan if it's warm, or grab an extra blanket if it's cold.

Commit to a relaxing bedtime routine. A nightly bath, 20 minutes of reading, or writing in a journal can help kids unwind and fall asleep.

No animals on the bed. Pets who sleep on the bed may stretch, change positions, or move around and wake your child up.

Countdown to sleep. Tell your child to try this mind-calming exercise: Start at 100 and count back to 1.

Other Common Side Effects

Some other possible effects include:

Nausea and headaches: ADHD drugs can make your child feel like they need to throw up. This side effect usually goes away after a few weeks. In the meantime, your child might feel better if they take their medicine with food.

Delayed growth: Some research shows that some children may grow more slowly than they should during their first year on ADHD medicine. But they seem to catch up during years 2 and 3. Kids who take breaks from ADHD drugs, like on weekends and during summer vacation, may not have this issue.

Sudden mood changes: Some children with ADHD get cranky when their drugs wear off. This is sometimes known as the rebound effect. It may mean the dose is too high or the medicine isn't right for your child. This may also be related to not having a way to expend their energy. Exercise will help with mood regulation.

Can You Treat ADHD Without Drugs?

For most families, that means the beginning of a long trek through the world of pharmaceuticals. Medications are the top treatment for ADHD, and they're effective for 80% of kids with the disorder.

But many parent's worry about side effects and want to exhaust every other option before they put their child on medicine.

No matter what your decision is, you can help your child live a calmer, more successful life.

To Medicate, or Not to Medicate?

For some, like Sonia, it was a matter of age. "My son was just 5 years old when he was diagnosed with ADHD, and I thought that was too young for medication," she says.

In fact, the American Academy of Pediatrics agrees. They almost always recommend that, before age 6, you start with behavior therapy.

"Parents often ask if they can try other treatments first before they turn to medication, and there are several methods that are effective," says Richard Gallagher, PhD, of the Institute for Attention Deficit Hyperactivity and Behavior Disorders at the NYU Child Study Center. He encourages parents to try other things while they look into the risks and benefits of medications.

Gallagher says that behavior changes alone are most effective with kids who are only inattentive and unfocused, rather than those who are also impulsive and hyperactive. The most successful treatment for ADHD combines both meds and behavior management.

Parent and Teacher Help

Parents and classroom teacher's play a starring role in helping a child learn to recognize and adjust their behavior, Gallagher says.

For parents, this means creating small, manageable goals for their child, such as sitting for 10 minutes at the dinner table, and then giving rewards for achieving them. It's also helpful for the teacher to send home a daily "report card," letting the parents know whether the child met their behavior goals at school that day.

From a young age, Sonia's son was graded in school every 20 minutes on three goals: staying seated, staying on task, and being respectful of others. His reward for meeting the goals were more time shooting hoops later in the day - a more effective strategy than punishing him for misbehaving, his mom says.

A coach or tutor can work with older children to come up with a system for keeping track of their books, papers, and assignments, says Edward Hallowell, MD, the author of Delivered from Distraction. "This is more helpful than Mom or Dad trying to help organize, because with a parent, it can come across as nagging," he says.

Sleep

Getting enough shut-eye can be a game-changer for kids with ADHD. Research shows that just an extra half-hour of sleep can help with restlessness and impulsivity.

"A lot of kids with ADHD also have sleep disorders, and each condition makes the other one worse," says Mark Stein, PhD, an ADHD specialist at the Seattle Children's Hospital.

One of the most common sleep issues for kids with ADHD is that they can't settle down and fall asleep; then their exhaustion the next day makes their symptoms worse. While some doctors recommend sleep aids such as melatonin, you should start by practicing good sleep habits:

Have a consistent bedtime, even on the weekend.

Keep the bedroom cool and dark.

Create a soothing winding-down ritual.

"We have bedtime broken down into 10 specific tasks, like taking a bath, putting on pajamas, reading for a half-hour," Sonia says. "He had trouble falling asleep before, but the routine really helps him settle down."

That also means no screens of any kind before bedtime. Take computers, TVs, phones, and video games out of the bedroom so your child isn't distracted or tempted.

Exercise

Make sure your child has plenty of opportunities to run and play (at appropriate times). Some recent studies found that after about 30 minutes of exercise, kids with ADHD can focus and organize their thoughts better.

Elise can confirm these results. "Like a lot of kids with ADHD, my son doesn't have very good coordination, but he's fallen in love with swimming," she says. "He enjoys the feel of the water and always feels calmer when he gets out of the pool."

If your child wants to play organized sports that require focus and concentration, like baseball or tennis, there's more to the equation. "Before they started medication, many of my patients were stuck playing the outfield, where they would just wander around chasing daisies," Stein says. "But the medication helped them play better and be part of the team."

Meditation and Mindfulness

A new line of research is exploring how mindfulness -- learning how to sharpen focus, raise awareness, and practice self-control through breathing and meditation -- may help manage the symptoms of ADHD.

One small study found that when both children and their parents completed an 8-week mindfulness-training program, the kids had fewer symptoms. And their parents felt less of the stress that typically comes with their role.

This is promising news, but Gallagher points out there isn't yet enough solid evidence to fully recommend the strategy.

Music Therapy

It can hone attention and strengthen social skills. It's rhythmic and structured. And playing music requires different parts of your brain to work together, as well as learning how to be a part of a group.

There's very little hard research specifically connecting music with ADHD symptoms, but scientists do know that when children play an instrument -- taking piano lessons at home, say, or playing cello with a school orchestra -- they do much better on tests of executive function than children who don't study music. That's the ability of the brain to organize and easily switch between tasks.

If your child would rather kick a soccer ball than pick up a flute, or can't sit still for lessons or practice, simply listening to their favorite playlist may calm them down long enough to finish their homework. When you listen to music you like, your brain releases dopamine, a chemical that also helps with focus.

More work needs to be done to connect ADHD to music, but it's certainly an area worth exploring, especially for music-loving families.

Omega-3 Fatty Acids

Over the years, several "ADHD diets" have been proposed and then dismissed by science. New research points to a connection between omega-3s and ADHD. These nutrients are found in fish such as salmon, in walnuts, flaxseeds, and soy products, in leafy greens, and in other foods. They're also available in over-the-counter supplements, as well as in the prescription Vayarin.

A study found that kids with ADHD have lower levels of omega-3s in their blood, which suggests bumping up the amount in their diet might reduce ADHD symptoms.

Although omega-3 supplements aren't widely recommended as a treatment, Hallowell points out that eating a balanced diet -- including fish, whole grains, and plenty of fruits and vegetables -- and cutting down on sugar and processed foods can certainly help your child live a healthier life.

9 Lifestyle Tips

These tips may help your child -- and you:

Join a support group. Organizations include Children and Adults with Attention-Deficit/Hyperactivity Disorder (CHADD).

Boost your child's self-esteem. Because a child with ADHD may have difficulty processing directions and other information, they may apt to be bombarded with corrections, leaving them with a low opinion of themselves. Do whatever you can to boost your child's self-esteem.

Praise and reward good behavior promptly.

Be consistent with discipline, and make sure other caregivers follow your methods.

Make instructions simple and specific ("Brush your teeth. Now, get dressed."), instead of general ("Get ready for school.").

Encourage your child's special strengths, particularly in sports and out-of-school activities.

Set and follow routines for meals, bedtime, play, and other activities.

Make time for play and exercise -- outside in a natural setting if possible. Don't let homework or screen time monopolize all of your child's time after school.

Simplify your child's room to minimize distractions, such as toys and improve organization.

Autism, also called autism spectrum disorder (ASD), is a complicated condition that includes problems with communication and behavior. It can involve a wide range of symptoms and skills. ASD can be a minor problem or a disability that needs full-time care in a special facility.

People with autism have trouble with communication. They have trouble understanding what other people think and feel. This makes it hard for them to express themselves, either with words or through gestures, facial expressions, and touch.

People with autism might have problems with learning. Their skills might develop unevenly. For example, they could have trouble communicating but be unusually good at art, music, math, or memory. Because of this, they might do especially well on tests of analysis or problem-solving.

More children are diagnosed with autism now than ever before. But the latest numbers could be higher because of changes in how it's diagnosed, not because more children have a disorder.

Autism Signs and Symptoms

Symptoms of autism usually appear before a child turns 3. Some people show signs from birth.

Common symptoms of autism include:

A lack of eye contact

A narrow range of interests or intense interest in certain topics

Doing something over and over, like repeating words or phrases, rocking back and forth, or flipping a lever

High sensitivity to sounds, touches, smells, or sights that seem ordinary to other people

Not looking at or listening to other people

Not looking at things when another person points at them

Not wanting to be held or cuddled

Problems understanding or using speech, gestures, facial expressions, or tone of voice

Talking in a sing-song, flat, or robotic voice

Trouble adapting to changes in routine

Some children with autism may also have seizures. These might not start until adolescence.

Autism Spectrum Disorders

These types were once thought to be separate conditions. Now, they fall under the range of autism spectrum disorders. They include:

Asperger's syndrome. These children don't have a problem with language; in fact, they tend to score in the average or above-average range on intelligence tests. But they have social problems and a narrow scope of interests.

Autistic disorder. This is what most people think of when they hear the word "autism." It refers to problems with social interactions, communication, and play in children younger than 3 years.

Childhood disintegrative disorder. These children have typical development for at least 2 years and then lose some or most of their communication and social skills.

Pervasive developmental disorder (PDD or atypical autism). Your doctor might use this term if your child has some autistic behavior, like delays in social and communications skills, but doesn't fit into another category.

Autism Causes

Exactly why autism happens isn't clear. It could stem from problems in parts of your brain that interpret sensory input and process language.

Autism is four times more common in boys than in girls. It can happen in people of any race, ethnicity, or social background. Family income, lifestyle, or educational level doesn't affect a child's risk of autism.

Autism runs in families, so certain combinations of genes may increase a child's risk.

A child with an older parent has a higher risk of autism.

Pregnant women who are exposed to certain drugs or chemicals, like alcohol or anti-seizure medications, are more likely to have autistic children. Other risk factors include maternal metabolic conditions such as diabetes and obesity. Research has also linked autism to untreated phenylketonuria (also called PKU, a metabolic disorder caused by the absence of an enzyme) and rubella (German measles).

There is no evidence that vaccinations cause autism.

Autism Screening and Diagnosis

It can be hard to get a definite diagnosis of autism. Your doctor will focus on behavior and development.

For children, diagnosis usually takes two steps.

A developmental screening will tell your doctor whether your child is on track with basic skills like learning, speaking, behavior, and moving. Experts suggest that children be screened for these developmental delays during their regular checkups at 9 months, 18 months, and 24 or 30 months of age. Children are routinely checked specifically for autism at their 18-month and 24-month checkups.

If your child shows signs of a problem on these screenings, they'll need a more complete evaluation. This might include hearing and vision tests or genetic tests. Your doctor might want to bring in someone who specializes in autism disorders, like a developmental pediatrician or a child psychologist. Some psychologists can also give a test called the Autism Diagnostic Observation Schedule (ADOS).

If you weren't diagnosed with autism as a child but notice yourself showing signs or symptoms, talk to your doctor.

Autism Treatment

There's no cure for autism. But early treatment can make a big difference in development for a child with autism. If you think your child shows symptoms of ASD, tell your doctor as soon as possible.

What works for one person might not work for another. Your doctor should tailor treatment for you or your child. The two main types of treatments are:

Behavioral and communication therapy to help with structure and organization. Applied Behavior Analysis (ABA) is one of these treatments; it promotes positive behavior and discourages negative behavior. Occupational therapy can help with life skills like dressing, eating, and relating to people. Sensory integration therapy might help someone who has problems with being touched or with sights or sounds. Speech therapy improves communication skills.

Medications to help with symptoms of ASD, like attention problems, hyperactivity, or anxiety.

Talk to your doctor before trying something different, like a special diet.

CONCLUSION

ADHD and ASD are lifelong conditions that can be managed with treatments that are right for the individual. Be patient and open to trying various treatments. You may also need to move to new treatments as your child gets older and symptoms evolve.

Scientists are continuing to research the connection between these two conditions. Research may reveal more information about the causes and more treatment options may become available.

Talk to your doctor about new treatments or clinical trials. If your child has been diagnosed with only ADHD or ASD and you think they may have both conditions, talk to your doctor. Discuss all your child's symptoms and whether your doctor thinks the diagnosis should be adjusted. A correct diagnosis is essential to receiving effective treatment.